Dear Daughter,

Live abundantly free.

A Devotional for Overcoming Your
Past Hurts, Habits and Fears.

For Mimi
my dear
daughter.
mom, Daddy
by Nov. 2020
reyna morris

To my husband, Christopher:
Your unconditional love introduced me to a God who heals and loves me even in my darkest moments. Thank you for allowing me to continue to share my past hurt in order to set other people free. I love you so much!

To my daughters, Ariana and Analise:
Your unconditional love has been a healing balm to my heart. You are a gift to us from the Lord above! Don't ever allow anyone to dim the light that is shining so bright inside of you. You two are world-changers! Dream big! We serve a mighty God!
Nothing is impossible with our God.

To His beloved daughters:
You matter to him, you are enough. He sees you, and He loves you even in your darkest moments. May you have eyes to see, ears to hear, a clear mind to accept, and a heart to receive His love letters.

"For nothing will be impossible with God." —Luke 1:37 ESV

This book is proof of His faithfulness.

Introduction

Dear Daughter was inspired by daily conversations I had with God. I experienced many hardships in my youth that caused my outlook on life to be negative. My life was chaotic and out of control. I had a lot to be thankful for, like being married to my husband who respected and loved me and being a mother to my beautiful daughters, but my battle was internal. My family, friends, and co-workers never noticed my mental health spiraling downward. I was depressed, anxious, and restless. But God... His thoughts were true, encouraging and life-giving. It was time for change. I was tired of living life as a victim. I was tired of settling for mediocrity. I knew deep down in my heart He had more for me. I began to guard my heart, for everything I did flowed from it. I was still enough to hear his audible voice and wrote down all He said. Dear Daughter was birthed through these continual conversations I had with my Heavenly Father. This moment was so monumental for me that I had to put a daily journaling section in this devotional for you as well. Feel free to use the space to write down the words, truth, vision, or promises that God speaks to you each day. My prayer is that it helps you open up and build an intimate relationship with your Heavenly Father.

His words, which sustained me, began to breathe life into my lungs. They gave purpose to my existence, carrying me through the valleys and to the mountaintops. One day at a time, they brought life to my dry bones and lifted my spirit. The heaviness began to lift off me. For the first time in my life I felt abundantly free. My life became colorful, abundant and overflowing. My purpose became clear to me and I felt alive. When the Lord spoke to me I couldn't keep it to myself. I felt the Lord wanting me to share it with all His daughters. These short letters are powerful, encouraging and liberating. They will walk you through a journey of learning to trust Him, while building an intimate relationship with the one who created you. They will lead you to an abundant life; a life of freedom.

Daddy, Abba, God, Holy Spirit, Prince of Peace, Lover of my soul—Jesus, He is all those things and more. Know who He is so that you can know who He is not. Then you will be able to turn off the lies of the enemy. You will know the truth and the truth will set you free. He loves you just the way you are; He knows where you are in your journey. Trust Him. Daily, He will lead you to quiet waters. He will speak directly to your heart, and He will renew your mind. If you surrender your life to Him, He will heal you, restore you, and set you free.

Dear Daughter,
are you ready to live set free?

*The scriptures I meditated on which inspired these love letters can be found in the NIV Bible.

The truth shall set you free.

John 8:32

DAY 1

Dear Daughter,

Listen. Listen. Listen. I am trying to speak to you, will you just listen my love. I am providing an opportunity for you to listen to my gentle whisper. I am taking distractions away from you so you can draw close to my mighty voice. In the stillness, I am there. My wholesome truth benefits those who will listen. Daughter, will you listen? Not everyone is listening. But you, I have designed you to listen if you choose to. In the stillness I want to whisper the purpose I have for your life. I want to share the needs I have for you to fulfill here on Earth. I want to give you an assignment that will help build others up. I want to show you the needs you can fulfill with my strength. Let my love fill you with my truth, speak wholesome, uplifting words that will be helpful to many. Build up my kingdom. Build a life that will honor me and share my persistent love. I know you are a great listener—Hear me, you are destined for greatness!

"Do not let any unwholesome talk come out of your mouths, but only what is helpful for building others up according to their needs, that it may benefit those who listen."
Ephesians 4:29 NIV

Dear Daughter,

_____

_____

_____

_____

_____

_____

_____

_____

_____

_____

_____

_____

_____

_____

_____

_____

DAY 2

Dear Daughter,

I made you with specific skills, talents and a unique personality. I did that on purpose so you can reach many. With those gifts, you will share my love with them in such a unique way that is tailored to you. This is why it's so important to stay true to yourself .You will reach them in ways no one else can. Stop playing small, stop hiding, worried about what others will think about the wonderful, powerful profound gift(s) I have given you. Instead of worrying about what others think about what I have blessed you with, use that energy to create something meaningful and impactful with eternal value. The gifts I gave you aren't meant to sit on a bookshelf and collect dust. They are meant to fill you with my presence so that it can align you with passion to pursue my will for your life. My will brings peace, purpose, zeal, joy, and prosperity into your life. These things will overflow and spill onto others and they will experience my sweet presence. So, stir up the gift of God. It's stir-up season!

"For this reason I remind you to fan into flame the gift of God, which is in you through the laying on of my hands."
2 Timothy 1:6 NIV

Dear Daughter,

_____

_____

_____

_____

_____

_____

_____

_____

_____

_____

_____

_____

_____

_____

_____

_____

DAY 3

Dear Daughter,

I created you for greatness. Why are you so afraid to follow your God-dream? Do you know who I am? I am your father, the one who created you; I am mighty, powerful and unstoppable. I love you more than you could ever comprehend. My love never falters. It is unfailing. Nothing can, or will, ever separate you from my love. Please, stop fearing—stop letting distractions from the outside world tell you what you can and cannot do. Come to me; learn from me, I will empower you to do all that I have called you to do. The fear that keeps hindering you from sharing your story is fear from the devil. He knows your story. It's a powerful one! I wrote it knowing that your voice will influence many. He knows that your story matters. He knows that many need to hear it, so that the chains can break from the bondage that is keeping them from their God-given destiny. Daughter, break every chain!

"The Spirit of the Sovereign Lord is on me, because the Lord has anointed me to proclaim good news to the poor. He has sent me to bind up the brokenhearted, to proclaim freedom for the captives and release from darkness for the prisoners."
Isaiah 61:1 NIV

Dear Daughter,

_____

_____

_____

_____

_____

_____

_____

_____

_____

_____

_____

_____

_____

_____

_____

_____

DAY 4

Dear Daughter,

I know everything about you...every detail, every thought and every desire in your heart. The deepest secrets, the lost dreams, your doubts. I know. Don't forget I created you, and everything I create is beautiful. I created you on purpose for a purpose. You are destined to create beautiful things. To make a difference in this world. Know that the process will be tough, and the opposition will try and squeeze everything out of you. The devil will try and stop you from sharing your beautiful gift with the world. Let me remind you that I have already won. Nobody can stop you from your God-given destiny. You are victorious, an overcomer and unstoppable, my daughter. I will never stop fighting for you! You are so precious to me.

"For you created my inmost being;
you knit me together in my mother's womb.
I praise you because I am fearfully and wonderfully made;
your works are wonderful, I know that full well."
Psalm 139:13-14 NIV

Dear Daughter,

_____

_____

_____

_____

_____

_____

_____

_____

_____

_____

_____

_____

_____

_____

_____

_____

_____

_____

_____

DAY 5

Dear Daughter,

The enemy tried to destroy you at such a young age. He knew you were destined for greatness. What I have instilled in you, nobody else has! You are unique, one of a kind, lover of my soul, creative, passionate, adventurous, a dreamer, a doer, wise, gentle, kind, loving, God-fearing, ambitious, a peacemaker with a big servant heart; you are an encourager, a world changer and I love that about you! I created you like that on purpose, for a purpose! Walk confidently in it. Don't shy away. It's time to shine. Shine bright so that everyone can see my glory!

"The thief comes only to steal and kill and destroy; I have come that they may have life, and have it to the full."
John 10:10 NIV

Dear Daughter,

_____

_____

_____

_____

_____

_____

_____

_____

_____

_____

_____

_____

_____

_____

_____

_____

_____

_____

DAY 6

Dear Daughter,

There is nothing you can't accomplish with my strength. Always remember that in life there will be many ideas, dreams, visions that I give you. People will not understand or believe you. They don't have to get it. Just like Noah, when He faithfully, obediently created the Ark. I gave him a vision, He heard my voice, I told him the dimensions, the style, and some of the details, and I led him. In my time, the vision unfolds. He was faithful so I rewarded him, and He inherited an abundant life. He deserved it. You deserve it. Will you trust that I can do more than you can ever imagine?

"Now to him who is able to do immeasurably more than all we ask or imagine, according to his power that is at work within us."
Ephesians 3:20 NIV

Dear Daughter,

_____
_____
_____
_____
_____
_____
_____
_____
_____
_____
_____
_____
_____
_____
_____
_____
_____

DAY 7

Dear Daughter,

Walk in the power of the Holy Spirit. I have given you authority over all the earth, and over every creeping thing that creeps upon the earth. My spirit is powerful it can destroy strongholds. My love will lead you to freedom. It is more potent than anything I've ever created. *It heals all wounds.* Those wounds and scars that still remain, my love heals. Don't think I have forgotten you. I was there with you, and always will be. I've never left you nor forsaken you. It's time. Healing is yours! Will you choose to spend time with your first love? I am the way, the truth and the life. Be still, lean into my truth. I promise to set you *free.*

"Jesus answered, 'I am the way and the truth and the life.
No one comes to the Father except through me.'"
John 14:6 NIV

Dear Daughter,

_____

_____

_____

_____

_____

_____

_____

_____

_____

_____

_____

_____

_____

_____

_____

_____

Give me all
the broken
pieces I will
heal &
restore you.

- God

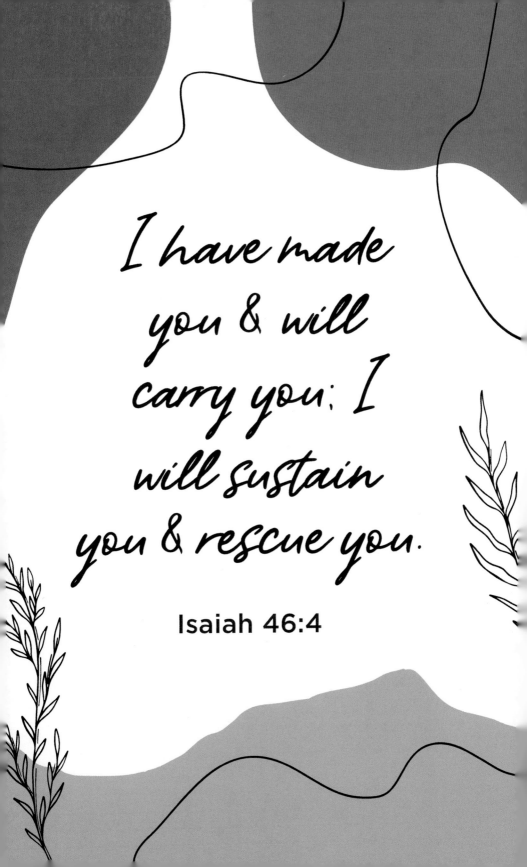

I have made you & will carry you; I will sustain you & rescue you.

Isaiah 46:4

DAY 8

Dear Daughter,

I promise you a sound mind all the days of your life. If you choose to follow me and know my voice you will walk *in your destiny.*

Don't let your limited thinking stop you from believing in what I can do with your life. You can create anything that I've placed on your heart to do. Stop limiting me. I am big—bigger than you can ever comprehend. Don't limit what you can do in my presence. Remember, all things are possible with God to the one who believes. Daughter, do you still believe? If not, will you believe? I have so much in store for the believer, *you!* Tap into my voice and I will lead you to create great meaningful things. I'm speaking to you now. Will you listen? What you will create will leave an eternal mark.

"Blessed is she who has believed that the Lord would fulfill his promises to her!"
Luke 1:45 NIV

Dear Daughter,

_____

_____

_____

_____

_____

_____

_____

_____

_____

_____

_____

_____

_____

_____

_____

_____

DAY 9

Dear Daughter,

There is power in the words you tell yourself. Life and death is in the power of the tongue. Focus on the good; keep your eyes on me and all that I have blessed you with. Start with what's in front of you. Call out the abundant blessings. Cultivate a thankful heart so that your body will overflow with joy. Joy is found in lenses of gratitude. Gratitude transforms hearts. Your smile will radiate a powerful light. A light that radiates something special, many will want to know where it's coming from.

"The tongue has the power of life and death, and those who love it will eat its fruit."
Proverbs 18:21 NIV

Dear Daughter,

_____

_____

_____

_____

_____

_____

_____

_____

_____

_____

_____

_____

_____

_____

_____

_____

DAY 10

Dear Daughter,

Why do you allow your mind to wander? Why do you allow other people's fears to stir your emotions? Allowing doubt to creep into the cracks of your fragile heart. Guard your heart, daughter, for everything you do flows from it. I am the same yesterday, today and tomorrow. Keep your mindset on the only one that is truly constant. Where I am, there is constant peace. Where I am, there is eternal joy. There is no room for fear or worry. I am your prince of peace, I am your joy! I am your constant answer. The solution to all your hidden concerns, fears and worries is being in *my presence*!

"Above all else, guard your heart, for everything you do flows from it."
Proverbs 4:23 NIV

Dear Daughter,

_____

_____

_____

_____

_____

_____

_____

_____

_____

_____

_____

_____

_____

_____

_____

_____

_____

_____

DAY 11

Dear Daughter,

I often find you burdened, exhausted, and weary. Trying to carry the world's problems on your shoulders. Your mind is on overdrive trying to solve problems that are mine to solve. Let go of trying to control everything around you. It's okay to rest, to not have to figure it all out. I am for you and not against you. Your restless spirit keeps trying to take back the burdens you once released to me. You go from feeling light one day, to heavy the next and repeat. Feeling like there is no light at the end of the tunnel. I didn't design you to be a carrier of burdens. I designed you to be a carrier of hope. Remember, my yoke is easy and my burden is light. Will you release all your burdens back to me for good? I am the one with the strong shoulders—I carry the world. I created it.

"Come to me, all you who are weary and burdened,
and I will give you rest."
Matthew 11:28 NIV

Dear Daughter,

_____

_____

_____

_____

_____

_____

_____

_____

_____

_____

_____

_____

_____

_____

_____

DAY 12

Dear Daughter,

There is hope in the breaking. Hope in the sorrow. Fix your eyes on hope. Stop looking at the pain. The vivid memories of the past, Satan wants you to replay in your mind, so that you remain bounded. Yes, you are saved but bounded is not truly free. In my presence, you are complete, not lacking anything. Only with the power of the Holy Spirit are you able to forgive. It's time. Time to let go of the past that hinders you from my ultimate purpose. Open up your hands. Trust me with the burdens. You weren't meant to carry that kind of weight. Surrender your strongholds to me. I will renew your strength. I will set you free!

"But those who hope in the Lord will renew their strength. They will soar on wings like eagles; they will run and not grow weary, they will walk and not be faint."
Isaiah 40:31 NIV

Dear Daughter,

_____

_____

_____

_____

_____

_____

_____

_____

_____

_____

_____

_____

_____

_____

_____

_____

_____

DAY 13

Dear Daughter,

Stop resenting your story. I wrote it. I have a plan to use it for my good. I am the author of your life. I don't make any mistakes. Your story is one of many stories that I **heal**. But only if you let me use your pain will people experience my power through you. The Spirit of God will heal many. Stop running; you can't hide because I designed you to shine bright, so many can see me in your life. Yield to me, my daughter, allow me to use you as an example of my redemption power! For the first time, many will feel seen, noticed and loved. They will meet their Savior—their *first love*. There is power in your story, don't ever dilute it. My child, your story radiates—strength, *overcomer and victory!*

"And we know that in all things God works for the good of those who love him, who have been called according to his purpose."
Romans 8:28 NIV

"The word of the Lord came to me saying, 'Before I formed you in the womb I knew you, before you were born I set you apart; I appointed you as a prophet to the nations.'"
Jeremiah 1:4-5 NIV

Dear Daughter,

_____

_____

_____

_____

_____

_____

_____

_____

_____

_____

_____

_____

_____

_____

_____

_____

DAY 14

Dear Daughter,

I forgive you, so please forgive yourself for the mistake(s) that you made. Stop holding yourself in bondage. I freed you when you accepted me as your Savior. So why are you still living as if you are in bondage? Why are you still carrying this baggage around? Why are you allowing it to bleed into all the relationships I have blessed you with? I desire for you to live in total freedom. I didn't design you to live bound by your past. Let go of the dreams that haunt you. Surrender them to me. When you hold on to things, I can't work in those areas of your life. I want to make you a vessel in which my love and grace overflows through you to those who are hurting—to those who are bound by their sins and past mistakes like you once were. Daughter, with that love, set people *free*.

"For it is by grace you have been saved, through faith—and this is not from yourselves, it is the gift of God—"
Ephesians 2:8 NIV

Dear Daughter,

_____

_____

_____

_____

_____

_____

_____

_____

_____

_____

_____

_____

_____

_____

_____

_____

You are worthy
of wonderful
things, but
first you must
believe.

Don't give up before the breakthrough happens.

DAY 15

Dear Daughter,

When you learn to forgive yourself, you will be able to forgive others. That is my will for you. You are in my presence when you forgive others. When I look at you, I don't remember your sins. So please stop replaying your sins, my precious daughter. A sin is a sin; I don't look at one any greater than the other. I love you. I have always loved you. Nothing will keep you from my eternal love. I know you were in pain when you made those mistakes. I saw your heart. It was in pain. I saw it bleeding. Know that even though you felt alone, you were never alone. I was there by your side, every step of the way. I always have been, and I always will be, there for you. Now, let those that hurt you free, release them to God, forgive them for the pain they caused you. Stop allowing them to have power over your life. Stop expecting anything in return. Stop letting them determine your freedom. There is no need to wait for their apology. Beloved, move forward with your life. Stop living stuck as if my freedom on the cross wasn't enough. What I did on the cross was not just for everyone else. It was also for you. You matter to me! Every detail in your life matters to me. The pain you keep replaying keeps you from receiving my full love for you. It keeps you from wholeheartedly trusting me. Will you trust me so that you can learn to trust again? Will you come back to my pure heart? Will you stop running from me? I want to give you the tools to live your best life. My word is true. Allow it to save you. Set yourself free from unforgiveness. Don't allow it to be spiritual cancer to your spirit. Keeping you from connecting with God. Choose forgiveness so you can be whole, my daughter. My desire is for you to live free indeed.

"Bear with each other and forgive one another if any of you has a grievance against someone. Forgive as the Lord forgave you."
Colossians 3:13 NIV

Dear Daughter,

_____

_____

_____

_____

_____

_____

_____

_____

_____

_____

_____

_____

_____

_____

_____

_____

DAY 16

Dear Daughter,

Why are you so hard on yourself? Criticizing my beautiful creations and constantly striving for perfection. Obsessing to always have everything right. I'm here to remind you there is beauty in the imperfection. There is a story to be told in every mistake, chip and broken heart. Don't miss out on great relationships because you can't see past the flaws. People can relate more to those that are real with their struggles. Those that display my grace. Most importantly, don't miss out on a relationship with me. *I love you just the way you are!* You don't have to be perfect to be in my presence. So stop waiting for the perfect moment, season, situation. Do it afraid. Come as you are. Even in your brokeness I will love you. While here on Earth, nobody will ever reach perfection. I designed life that way so that they would need the only one who is perfect and whole—*me!* In the eyes of my Father, I am perfect, so in the eyes of your Heavenly Father, you are perfect.

"But God demonstrates his own love for us in this: While we were still sinners, Christ died for us."
Romans 5:8 NIV

Dear Daughter,

_____

_____

_____

_____

_____

_____

_____

_____

_____

_____

_____

_____

_____

_____

_____

_____

DAY 17

Dear Daughter,

Don't lose your hope just because others around you are wavering. Hope in me, the one who is unfailing. I started this dream in you so I will sustain you. I will direct every one of your footsteps. I will take you through the process. Embrace the journey, my daughter. There is so much beauty in the process. Don't worry how it will all unfold. Trust in my guidance. Hope is built from your character. Who are you becoming in the process, daughter? Who do you allow to speak into your life? Where does your mind wander when doubt creeps in? Do you listen to the dream crushers or do you lean on the dream defenders? You must believe in yourself before others can believe in you. Not everyone will be for you, but I will always be on your side. I will never turn my heart from you. Daughter, I am your number one fan. I am your dream defender!

"Not only so, but we also glory in our sufferings, because we know that suffering produces perseverance; perseverance, character; and character, hope. And hope does not put us to shame, because God's love has been poured out into our hearts through the Holy Spirit, who has been given to us."
Romans 5:3-5 NIV

Dear Daughter,

_____
_____
_____
_____
_____
_____
_____
_____
_____
_____
_____
_____
_____
_____
_____
_____
_____

DAY 18

Dear Daughter,

You always believe I can do miracles for others, but doubt I can do them for you. Do you know that you matter to me? You are my pride and joy. I created you in my image and likeness, so beautiful and so wonderful. My word is your spiritual alignment. Don't let your emotions and thoughts weigh you down. Focus on my word and the miracle will come. If you're struggling with depression, I want to heal you. If you feel anxious, I want to bring peace to you. If you're grieving, I want to fill you with joy. I can bring dead things to life. I can supply all your needs. I can do things that are impossible to man. But for me nothing is impossible! Don't let your circumstance define what you believe. Let my word define your circumstance. Continue to *believe* in my word. My word is medicine for your soul, mind and body. You know where to find me. If you've forgotten, I'm just a prayer away. You will find me when you seek me with your whole heart.

"You will seek me and find me when you seek me with
all your heart."
Jeremiah 29:13 NIV

Dear Daughter,

_____

_____

_____

_____

_____

_____

_____

_____

_____

_____

_____

_____

_____

_____

_____

_____

_____

DAY 19

Dear Daughter,

You desire a companion that will always have a listening ear. One who will encourage you when you feel like giving up. You desire a companion who will guide you when you feel lost and restore you when you feel broken. He must be confident when you're confused and able to make wise decisions. You desire him to be filled with zeal and step right in when you feel depleted. You desire one who never walks away and is present. He is constant and never backs away. He will comfort you when you feel afraid. He will always bring peace to the relationship. He will supply your every need. That companion you're looking for is me! When facing trials and difficulties, I will be all those things to you! No one can ever fill you up or provide like I can. My presence will come more alive to you as you draw closer to me. I can be all those things to you if you allow me. Daughter, who do you think I am? **If you believe I am who I say I am then you will experience my presence to the fullest.** Do not focus on who others say I am, but on whom my word says I am. Can I be all these things to you?

"God said to Moses, I am who I am. This is what you are to say to the Israelites: 'I am has sent me to you.'"
Exodus 3:14 NIV

Dear Daughter,

DAY 20

Dear Daughter,

I have not given you a spirit of fear, but of power, love and a sound mind. I see you continuing to struggle with the spirit of fear. You worry about things that will never happen, using up the mental energy you need in order to build beautiful life-giving things. Fear will lie to you. It will paralyze you if you allow yourself to fall into its trap. The enemy likes to distract my world-changers with fear so that it can delay them from creating change in this world. Don't allow Satan to cripple you nor steal your heart's desires. Remember, Satan is a thief and a liar. He desires to destroy the dreams you keep hidden in your heart. Don't allow other people's fears to stop you from following my voice. My voice is gentle, peaceful, true and filled with power. Know my truth so you can discern my voice from Satan. The Spirit of the Lord is on you, my daughter. I have anointed you to proclaim freedom to the prisoners, to set the oppressed free. But first you most walk in freedom from your past hurts, habits and addictions. It's time to let go of the spirits that have gripped you for many years—generations upon generations—strongholds. It's time. You, my darling, will break generational patterns. The patterns end with you! You are a chain-breaker! No longer a slave to your past sin. You are set free! Now you can yield and allow me to use you to set other people free! I want to affirm you that you are brave, courageous, fierce, determined, unstoppable, a go-getter, a doer of my word. I don't compare you to anyone, beloved. Run your race with holy confidence that you have been set free! My power forever lives in you. My love cast out all fear. So cling to me and I will show you how to live the abundant life!

"For the Spirit God gave us does not make us timid, but gives us power, love and self-discipline."
2 Timothy 1:7 NIV

Dear Daughter,

_____

_____

_____

_____

_____

_____

_____

_____

_____

_____

_____

_____

_____

_____

_____

_____

DAY 21

Dear Daughter,

Obeying my word will lead you to a blessed life. Do you remember the last thing I asked of you? Many of my daughters want my promises but they don't want the responsibility. *Obeying me will lead you to a satisfying life.* Store my commandments deep in your heart. Your heart is a sacred place. Satan cannot steal what is rightfully yours—peace and prosperity will follow you when you obey my command. Obey every single word that is written in my book. Do everything with your whole heart. Be all in. Don't be afraid to commit to getting to know me. Make time for me so you can know my will for your life. I desire for you to think about me all day long as I think about you. When you walk confidently in the next thing I asked you to do, your blessing will follow. I can't wait to bless you.

"My son, do not forget my teaching, but keep my commands in your heart, for they will prolong your life many years and bring you peace and prosperity."
Proverbs 3:1-2 NIV

Dear Daughter,

_____

_____

_____

_____

_____

_____

_____

_____

_____

_____

_____

_____

_____

_____

_____

_____

_____

You're so loved apart from what you do.

You are capable my daughter.

- God

DAY 22

Dear Daughter,

Who told you it was time to give up? Satan celebrates when you give up. "'Give up' weren't my final words on the cross." "It is finished" were my final words. So finish the race I called you to. There is a sudden change that is going to happen. Abundance is coming. Clarity is coming. But in order to finish this race strong, you must align your thoughts with my thoughts. Every morning say, "Your thoughts not my thoughts," "Your will not my will Lord." Ask yourself, "Are my thoughts destructive or constructive?" Do you tend to be negative or positive? I have given you the authority to control your thought life. Choose right thinking instead of stinking thinking. Guard your mind from hurtful, unhealthy media. Set boundaries with those who are toxic and serenity robbers. Meditate on things that are true, noble, right, pure, lovely, admirable, excellent, or praiseworthy. God's instruction manual "The Bible" will keep you aligned in His truth. Do not let go of my truth. Have a discerning heart, my daughter. Seek knowledge so you can live out my good, pleasing and perfect will.

"Finally, brothers and sisters, whatever is true, whatever is noble, whatever is right, whatever is pure, whatever is lovely, whatever is admirable—if anything is excellent or praiseworthy—think about such things."
Philippians 4:8 NIV

Dear Daughter,

_____

_____

_____

_____

_____

_____

_____

_____

_____

_____

_____

_____

_____

_____

_____

_____

_____

_____

DAY 23

Dear Daughter,

I will lead you to the Jordan River, but it's your choice to walk through it. It will require you to leave your old ways, old patterns, and habits of living. Walk through the unknown and into the promise land, daughter. It willtake trust, obedience and faith to walk in courage into the Promised Land. Not everyone will walk through it and get to the other side. But you, my darling, you are a natural born leader. I need you to be a leader before anyone sees you as one. I destined you for greatness! Don't let your past distort the blessings I have in front of you. Instead of doubt, remember my faithfulness rather than your past. Stop looking back. Leave the past hurt, pain, sin, and yoke of slavery behind you. Instead, lean forward. Trust me. Allow me to turn your wounds into scars, and your scars into something beautiful. Hurt people hurt people, and healed people heal people. Which do you want to be? This is the difference from living in your past and living in my presence. Will you trust me in the unknown and cross over into the Promised Land? Together, we will fight forward.

"Brothers and sisters, I do not consider myself yet to have taken hold of it. But one thing I do: Forgetting what is behind and straining toward what is ahead, I press on toward the goal to win the prize for which God has called me heavenward in Christ Jesus."
Philippians 3:13-14 NIV

Dear Daughter,

_____

_____

_____

_____

_____

_____

_____

_____

_____

_____

_____

_____

_____

_____

_____

DAY 24

Dear Daughter,

A controlling behavior leaves no room for me to operate in your life. I know the illusion of control has brought you comfort for many years, but it has also kept you from reaching your destiny. It's time, daughter, to exercise faith in me. Allow faith to operate in your life. One day at a time, all your dreams will unfold, your finances will follow, and your family will come to know their Savior. Surrender the need to control. The root of wanting to control everything around you is fear of the unknown, lack in trusting the one who created you detail by detail. Are you ready to trust me completely with your whole heart? I need your roots to be deeply grounded so when I bless you abundantly you are unshakeable. Your roots should be grounded in my unshakeable love. Have confidence in the one who created you. Exercise your faith one day at a time and trust will follow. You will grow intimately in me and then you will know that I want nothing but the best for you. You are significant in my eyes!

"Trust in the Lord with all your heart and lean not on your own understanding; in all your ways submit to him, and he will make your paths straight."
Proverbs 3:5-6 NIV

Dear Daughter,

_____

_____

_____

_____

_____

_____

_____

_____

_____

_____

_____

_____

_____

_____

_____

_____

_____

DAY 25

Dear Daughter,

The battle is not yours, it's mine. When you realize that, you will be able to stand confidently in full surrender—resting in me alone! When I ask you to rest, I am asking you to trust in me. When you trust me, worry bows down, fear bows down, sickness bows down, anxiety bows down, depression bows down, loneliness bows down, suicidal thoughts bow down, doubt bows down to the one that has all authority and power. Jesus Christ! Align yourself with me, daughter, and you will walk in full confidence. I have instilled in you the authority to rebuke the enemy's lies. When the enemy wants to distract you with destructive thoughts, tell him out loud, "That's a lie!" I demand you to flee in the name of Jesus! Get under my feet, Satan; you have no place in my thoughts, mind, body or spirit. You have no power or authority over my life. I am whole and I walk in certainty of which I am, and whose I am! No weapon shall be formed against me nor shall prosper. In Jesus' mighty name, Amen!

"No weapon forged against you will prevail, and you will refute every tongue that accuses you. This is the heritage of the servants of the Lord, and this is their vindication from me, declares the Lord."
Isaiah 54:17 NIV

Dear Daughter,

_____

_____

_____

_____

_____

_____

_____

_____

_____

_____

_____

_____

_____

_____

_____

_____

_____

_____

DAY 26

Dear Daughter,

Focus on the work that I have for you. I have chosen you to do special work in my kingdom. Ask yourself: What is special about me? What group of people has God called me to influence? What gifts has God placed in me? What value can I bring to someone's life? Daughter, know your mission. When you know your mission, you will know your purpose, and then you will know your people. When you have the right vision, prosperity will follow. My puzzle pieces will begin to form a beautiful picture. Believe in yourself and believe in your God. Together we can do all things! You are unstoppable, a force to be reckoned with. Don't be silent any longer. Be bold. Be brave. Be you. Walk in the awareness that your identity is in Christ. Move in the Spirit. Nothing can ever come against you. Walk confidently in your identity. Make no apologies, for I chose you for such a time as this. Shine bright, daughter! Illuminate this place.

"For if you remain silent at this time, relief and deliverance for the Jews will arise from another place, but you and your father's family will perish. And who knows but that you have come to your royal position for such a time as this?"
Ester 4:14 NIV

Dear Daughter,

_____

_____

_____

_____

_____

_____

_____

_____

_____

_____

_____

_____

_____

_____

_____

_____

_____

DAY 27

Dear Daughter,

I want to heal you. I desire for you to be whole and set free! I want to hand you the keys to your man-made prison door. The keys are my living word. But you must want it for yourself—freedom! Freedom is a choice. I offer it to every single soul. What's holding you back? What are you so afraid of? What is the one area of your life that you keep burying six feet deep? Bring that to the light. Let me free you from that stronghold, addiction, obsession and bondage. Let me remind you that when I died on the cross, I died for you! That means you aren't lacking, missing anything, or broken anymore. Your identity is found in Christ. You are worthy, you are whole, you are free, you are enough and you are *forgiven*. Lean on my living word, daughter. Believe in my word for the **truth sets people free**.

"To the Jews who had believed him, Jesus said, 'If you hold to my teaching, you are really my disciples. Then you will know the truth, and the truth will set you free.'"
John 8:31-32 NIV

Dear Daughter,

_____

_____

_____

_____

_____

_____

_____

_____

_____

_____

_____

_____

_____

_____

_____

_____

_____

_____

DAY 28

Dear Daughter,

I want to deliver you from the things that are holding you back from your destiny. Will you have faith to move forward? Can you build the small things I have entrusted you with today? I want you to move one step at a time in faith and holy fear. Sometimes the things I ask of you year after year may sound insane to you, but I will continue to ask until you move forward in boldness and obedience. I want to hear an everlasting "yes" from your lips. I have plans to prosper you. Do everything with your whole heart, a heart that desires to please me. I want you fully restored, so that when it's time, I will reveal you to those around you. My people will grow while being in your presence. You will radiate my faithfulness. Don't doubt that I called you to greatness. I am building something great in you. Prosperity is yours, will you see it? Be faithful in the little, keep building what's right in front of you. An everlasting "yes" from you is what this world needs in order to experience my faithfulness.

"'For I know the plans I have for you,' declares the Lord, 'plans to prosper you and not to harm you, plans to give you hope and a future.'"
Jeremiah 29:11 NIV

Dear Daughter,

_____

_____

_____

_____

_____

_____

_____

_____

_____

_____

_____

_____

_____

_____

_____

_____

_____

Praise Him
in the
storm... He
is faithful.

I am your
1 dream
defender.

- God

DAY 29

Dear Daughter,

Don't bury the one word I gave you, daughter. Hold on to it with faith and holy fear. Trust me during the process. I can't bless what you won't build. Take that one word and build one day at a time. Trust in me; take my words seriously. I blessed you with gifts so that you can influence many around you. Stop hiding the wonderful gifts I have given you. At the end of this world, I will ask you if you built all that I asked you to build during your time here on Earth. I have given you the ability to dream and build. What a gift that is. Building my kingdom by using the many talents I gave you. Stay in awe of what I am doing, which is building something great through you! I *care* about your destiny, daughter. Walk with me closely. I will keep things out that were meant to harm you. I will elevate you to new spiritual levels. Lean on me—The *Master Builder*!

"He said to me: 'Solomon your son is the one who will build my house and my courts, for I have chosen him to be my son, and I will be his father.'"
1 Chronicles 28:6 NIV

Dear Daughter,

_____

_____

_____

_____

_____

_____

_____

_____

_____

_____

_____

_____

_____

_____

_____

_____

_____

DAY 30

Dear Daughter,

When you face storms in your life, remain hopeful, I am elevating you. There is always purpose to the pain you go through. The process refines you and helps you become the woman I need you to become. There are doors that I close because they are toxic and keep you from connecting with me. Will you move from those closed doors? I am keeping things out that aren't leading you towards the direction I have for you. Will you stop seeking those who continue to hurt you, those who are toxic and keep you from the abundant life I've called you to? What's driving you to do the things that are against my will? Come to me as you are. Don't run from me any longer. I want to build an intimate relationship with you. I have loved you with an everlasting love. Will you still love me even when you don't feel that I'm working in your life? I never turn my heart from you. But if you do, I am there waiting for you.

"He said, 'If you listen carefully to the Lord your God and do what is right in his eyes, if you pay attention to his commands and keep all his decrees, I will not bring on you any of the diseases I brought on the Egyptians, for I am the Lord, who heals you."
Exodus 15:26 NIV

"The Lord appeared to us in the past, saying: 'I have loved you with an everlasting love; I have drawn you with unfailing kindness.'"
Jeremiah 31:3 NIV

Dear Daughter,

_____
_____
_____
_____
_____
_____
_____
_____
_____
_____
_____
_____
_____
_____
_____
_____
_____
_____

No past is
too broken
for the
grace and
love of
Jesus.

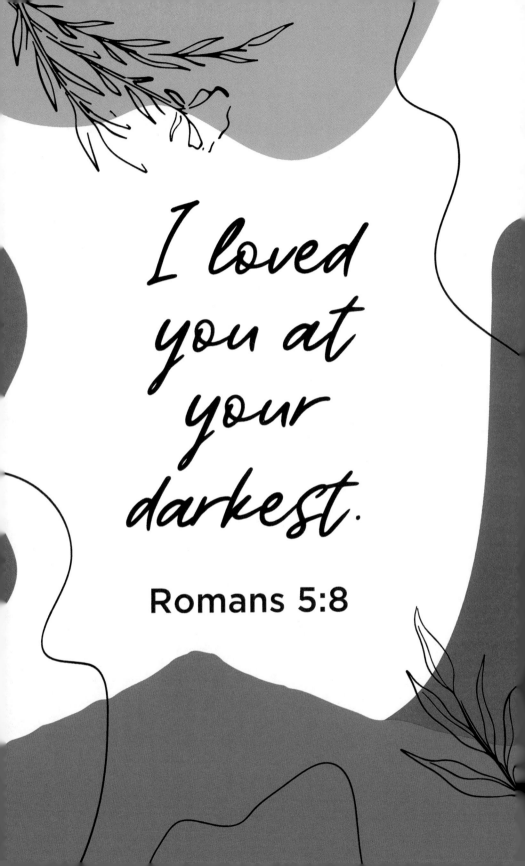

I loved you at your darkest.

Romans 5:8

You need only to **BE STILL.**

Exodus 14:14

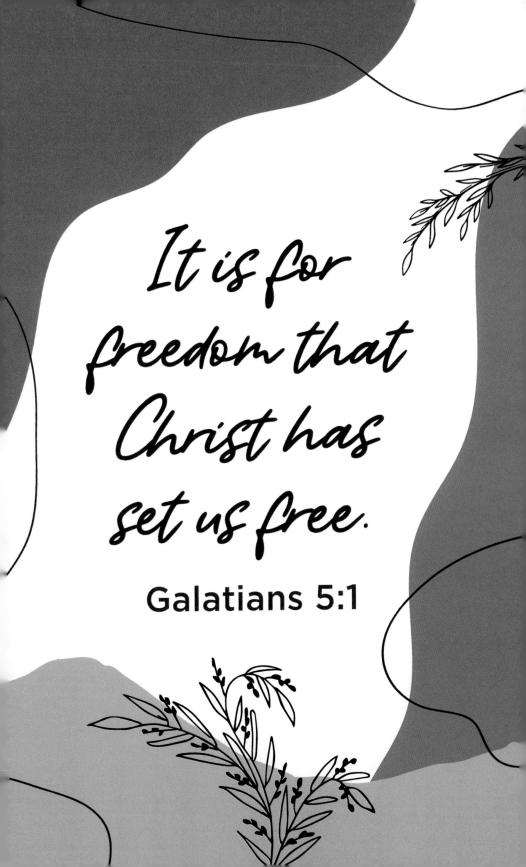

It is for freedom that Christ has set us free.

Galatians 5:1

Dear Daughter, I have loved you with
an everlasting love. With that love,
live abundantly free.

Acknowledgements

Thank you to Loureva for your willingness to always edit my work, and encouraging me on the fact that I had a gift to write.

Thank you to Becca for always being a listening ear, and for encouraging me that this was my season to write.

Thank you to Joane Casey for being my life coach through the writing process.

Thank you to Monica, Arleen, Isabel, Adina, Tiffany, Bethany, Diana Carreno, Stephanie, Patrice, Lina, Nayda, Gloria, Diana Ryan, Sera, Ella, Theresa, Graciela, Ananela, Elisa, Anjuli, Tami, Ashley, Jamie, Jennifer for always encouraging me to focus on the things of God.

Thank you to the women that influenced me to write my story: Ashley Abercrombie, Holly Wagner, Nicole Smithee, Bonnie Powell, Lara Casey, Lindsey Berteau, Harmony Dust Grillo, Christine Caine, and Joyce Meyer.

Thank you to Erika for the beautiful cover and graphic design, you are so talented!

Thank you to my dad and mom, Rolando and Celia; I thank you for your willingness to say yes to adopting me into your family, giving me the opportunity to have a better life and helping make me the woman I am today. To my sister, Cecy, for loving me unconditionally and accepting me as her one and only sister. I love you all!

Thank you to my mother-in-law, Annie Faye Morris, for always encouraging me, and being such a woman of faith in my life.

Made in the USA
Middletown, DE
19 November 2020